# COUNTRIES

# Poland

## Ruth Thomson

# Explore the world with **Popcorn -** your complete first non-fiction library.

Look out for more titles in the Popcorn range. All books have the same format of simple text and striking images. Text is carefully matched to the pictures to help readers to identify and understand key vocabulary. www.waylandbooks.co.uk/popcorn

First published in paperback in 2013 by Wayland

Wayland
Hachette Children's Books
338 Euston Road
London NW1 3BH

Wayland Australia
Level 17/207 Kent Street
Sydney NSW 2000

Produced for Wayland by
White-Thomson Publishing Ltd
www.wtpub.co.uk
+44 (0)843 208 7460

Editor: Steve White-Thomson
Designer: Amy Sparks
Picture researchers: Ruth Thomson/Steve White-Thomson
Series consultant: Kate Ruttle
Design concept: Paul Cherrill

British Library Cataloging in Publication Data
Thomson, Ruth, 1949-
   Poland -- (Countries)(Popcorn)
   1. Poland-- Juvenile literature
   I. Title II. Series
   914.3'8-dc22

ISBN: 978 0 7502 7196 7

Wayland is a division of Hachette Children's Books,
an Hachette UK company.
www.hachette.co.uk

Printed and bound in China

Picture Credits: Alamy: Paul Thompson Images front cover; Dreamstime: Sebastian Czapnik 11, Artur Ebrowski 18; Neil Thomson 23; Photolibrary: Frank Fell/The Travel Library 5, Egmont Strigl 14, Henryk T. Kaiser 15, 16; Shutterstock: puchan 1/19, Wiktor Bubniak 2/8, Kapa1966 6, Nightman1965 7, Tomasz Nieweglowski 9, Agata Dorobek 10, Wojciech Kozlowski 12, Marcin Niemiec 13, stormur 17tr, Elzbieta Sekowska 17tl, Krzysztof Slusarczyk 17br, Jaroslaw Grudzinski 17bl, ann&chris 20, EVRON 21

Every effort has been made to clear copyright. Should there be any inadvertent omission, please apply to the publisher for rectification.

#  Contents

# Where is Poland?

Here is a map of Poland. It is a
large country in Eastern Europe.

LITHUANIA

Baltic Sea

RUSSIA

Gdansk ○

Mazury Lakes

BELARUS

■ **Warsaw**

**POLAND**

GERMANY

River Oder

Sudeten Mountains

CZECH REPUBLIC

River Vistula

Krakow ○

Tatra Mountains

Carpathian Mountains

UKRAINE

▲ Mount Rysy

SLOVAK REPUBLIC

**EUROPE**

Warsaw is the capital city.

It is the biggest city in Poland.

The River Vistula flows through it.

Buildings in Warsaw town square were rebuilt after they were destroyed in World War II.

# Land and sea

Land in central Poland is flat. Hills and mountains stretch across the south. There are lakes and forests in the north.

There are more than 1,000 lakes in Poland.

Pine trees cover the lower slopes of the mountains.

Along the north of Poland is the Baltic Sea. The beaches are wide and sandy. Huge ships and ferries dock at several ports.

Tugs pull big ships into port.

# The weather

Poland has mild springs and warm summers. Sometimes there is heavy rain.

In summer, many people take trips to the mountains to walk and climb.

It is cold in winter. In the mountains, there is deep snow and cold frosts.

You must wrap up warm when you go out in the snow.

9

# Town and country

Towns have a market square in the centre, often with colourful old buildings. There are more modern buildings on the edge of towns.

*Town squares are often closed to traffic.*

There are many small
farms in the country.
Farmers mainly grow rye,
potatoes and cabbages.

Poland is
well-known
for its organic
vegetables.

Some small farms still use
horses to pull farm machines.

# Homes

In cities, there are many old housing estates with rows of tall blocks of flats. More colourful modern flats have green spaces, paths and shops nearby.

These flats have balconies where people can sit in good weather.

In the country, many old
houses are built of wood.
These are usually one-storey
high. Some have thatched roofs.

The people in this
house keep bees in
the straw beehive.

# Shopping

People shop for food in huge markets, supermarkets and small local shops.

People can buy tinned food and drinks in markets, as well as fruit and vegetables.

There are new shopping centres on the edges of cities. People shop here for clothes and household goods, such as saucepans and bedding.

Shopping centres stay open late, so people can visit them after work.

#  Food

Families eat their main meal together when everyone comes home from school and work.

Pork is roasted or made into ham or sausages.

People buy bread, hot dogs and other snacks from street stalls.

The most popular food in Poland is pork. Here are some of Poland's favourite foods.

pierogi
(stuffed dumplings)

borscht
(cold beetroot soup)

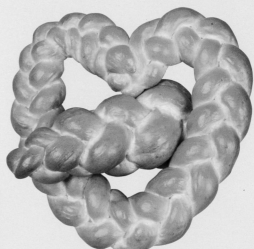

plaited bread

pork

# Sport

Football, swimming and horse riding are popular sports in Poland. People ride quad bikes along special tracks through forests and marshes.

Bends and humps in the tracks make quad biking exciting.

People canoe and kayak on the many lakes and rivers. In winter, they ski on the snowy mountain slopes.

Canoeists can paddle from one lake to another through canals.

# Holidays and festivals

Most Polish people are Roman Catholics. Many go to church on Sundays. Christmas and Easter are important religious celebrations.

At Easter, people paint or scratch patterns on the shell of hardboiled eggs.

In summer, there are folk festivals.
People wear colourful costumes and
parade through the streets. Dancers
perform to violin and accordion music.

All the costumes are
decorated with embroidery.

# Speak Polish!

**Cześć** (*ch-ay-esch*)                         Hello

**Do widzenia** (*do vee-dzeh-ya*)               Goodbye

**Proszę** (*pro-sheh*)                          Please

**Dziękuję** (*jen-koo-yek*)                     Thank you

**Tak** (*tak*)                                  Yes

**Nie** (*n-yeh*)                                No

**Nazywam się...** (*naz-i-vam sheh*)            My name is...

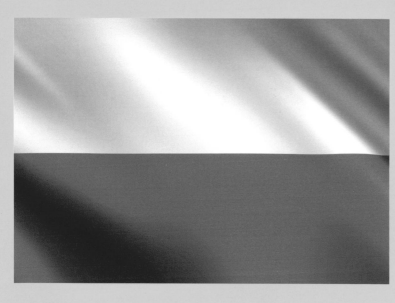

Red and white have been Poland's traditional colours for hundreds of years. White means peace. Red means bravery and strength.

# Make a Polish papercut

You will need:
• small piece of coloured paper
• scissors

In the past, Polish women made papercuts to decorate their homes. They glued these on to the walls, windows and furniture.

1. Fold the piece of paper in half.

fold

2. Cut a shape along the unfolded edge, through both layers of paper.

3. Cut little snips on all sides of your shape.

4. Open out your finished papercut.

# Glossary

**accordion** a musical instrument with a small keyboard and a folding box that you squeeze in and out to play

**capital** the city in a country where the government is

**embroidery** patterned stitching with colourful threads

**estate** a large area with lots of houses or flats on it

**folk festival** an event that shows off the music, dance and costumes of a country

**Roman Catholic** a Christian whose spiritual leader is the Pope in Rome

**thatched** covered with straw or reeds as a roof

# Index